The Simplified World

Petra White was born in Adelaide in 1975 and has lived since 1998 in Melbourne, where she works in a government department and is studying for a Master of Public Policy and Management. Her first book of poetry, *The Incoming Tide*, was shortlisted for the Queensland Premier's Prize and the ACT Poetry Prize.

The Simplified World

PETRA WHITE

JOHN LEONARD PRESS

First published 2010 by
John Leonard Press
PO Box 443, St Kilda, VIC 3182

National Library of Australia
Cataloguing-in-Publication data:

White, Petra, 1975 –.
The simplified world

ISBN 978 098 052 69 81
1. Title.
A821.4

Design: Sophie Gaur
Photo: Alex Matthews
Printed and bound by BPA Print Group, Burwood, Victoria

Set in Bembo

ACKNOWLEDGEMENTS

Poems in this collection have appeared in the *Age*, *Blast: Poetry and Critical Writing*, *Heat*, *The Best Australian Poems 2009* (ed. Robert Adamson, Black Inc.), *The Best Australian Poetry 2009* (ed. Alan Wearne, UQP), *The Puncher & Wattmann Anthology of Australian Poetry* (ed. John Leonard, 2009) and *Take Five 08* (ed. Adrian Caesar, Shoestring Press UK, 2009).

I am grateful to Elizabeth Campbell, L K Holt, Rick Johnson, Peter Naish and John Leonard. Many of these poems were begun at Hawthornden Castle International Retreat for Writers, where I was a Fellow in September 2008.

For

ELLIE,

MARTY,

LILI

&

ALEX

CONTENTS

Woman and Dog

A woman and a dog walked all day
beside the non-moving canal.
People who walk dogs displace themselves:

the dog sniffs and leads, harnesses
a human soul, spirit and flesh
willing or not. Its human-dog eyes

cradle the walkable world – a happy place –
a brimming here-and-yet. The canal
neither followed nor lagged behind.

There was the simplified world, on either side, green
fields and red houses. There was the little pub
they always got to.

So long they trudged, two bodies and one
soul, so many miles,
the paws began to bleed.

Little flecks of ruby blood glittered the black
rubbery pads, as if the dog was inking out
all the sadness of the woman.

And the woman, being just strong enough,
gathered up the dog (not a small one)
and carried it all the way home, wherever that was.

St Kilda

I

Sleepless seagulls fleer under floodlights,
they are caught like souls in light as in a net,
thoroughly winging their ways
around and through a day-dreamt freedom.
In a practice leap from love you stand
nowhere-they-can-find-me, bare feet in sand,
imagining a perfect loneliness, the soul a
self-stolen ship, breathing around the coast,
horizon-close, or sliding into darknesses
too vast for you to manage, depths too deep;
and then you want a cage of light, a finite hug
to swing you back to shore. The tidy beach,
a sliver of world, blinks its toy lighthouse,
something cries, 'come home, come home'.

2

Stripped to the soul, squatting at the shoreline,
thoughts prey like sharks but never bite,
no voice inside your skull sounds right.
O listen to the tiny waves crash their hardest,
as a lap-dog yaps its loudest to be loud.
Pitched past pitch of grief: how far is that?
Easy as tides, tears ride out, words are water . . .
there is blankness wide as the long sea.
Nor be consoled nor fear. Let down your tangle
of worries, wash them in salt as wounds
like to be washed. Say you are the furthest-
out fool, lost beyond losing. Sing, and sing,
but stay where you are and wait to be found,
sleeplessly smiling (at grief!) in the floodlight.

Older Sister

Deputy-mother of her maybe rivals,
love swings on and off.
Mary Poppins, Miss Hannigan,
spit-spot and slap-slap.

When parents say, she is shot like a comet
into adultness, to govern babies or keep
the ship of housework sailing.
Larger than adult, smaller than child,

chore-hungry and chore-fed,
a machine-child sweating at the iron.
Her fingers fly, her eyes are stone;
a ghost to herself, she body-and-soul becomes

the order that sorts the washing,
shyly perfecting the nappy's origami,
pressing the fatherly hankies
into high-piled civil squares.

On the floor, four toddlers sprawl
like dropped grenades: stilled by *Babar,*
that delicate French family of bourgeois-
monarch elephants and mint-

green apple-studded trees that float
through the screen and fill the timber house
that noses at the sky like Noah's Ark,
its cargo more than all the world.

It is like an order she has made:
four sisters, their hair still gleaming
in the braids she yanked into shape that morning.
Their future tantrums wait inside her throat,

she swallows them and keeps the peace.
The house teeters, creaks.
She slips out, climbs the voiceless apple tree,
squats quiet as a dove that ate the olive branch.

The babies drift by like clouds, their smiles
strung with cosmic spittle: she crouches,
a monster, hardened and un-hardened,
forming and re-forming,

eyes red with metamorphosis,
deep in the smell of feathers, wing-wax,
whirring breath,
she leaps from the apple tree,

lands in the kitchen, an angel,
and like four little kittens, the children
curl around her silk-slippered feet:
she pours them 'baby tea' – six sugars, all milk.

Ode to Coleridge

Feeling around in the human,
as if inside a sack, soul fends for itself,
fends off, prunes, cultivates,
eliminates,
makes itself up, says
'is this right?'
(and tries to be reasonably consistent)

tending itself, lurches like Sisyphus
into forwardness, backwardness,
urges itself to form a comma,
something next, next,
please move along now, please,
same again thanks,
as usual.

Dialogues of Soul and Body
seem bureaucratically polite.
The one complains of being chained by the other,
much like the married,
each certain of its own bounds.
What is darkness,
where does it come from?

Heavy as our fleshload,
weightless
as petals.
Here comes the train in the tunnel
(a cold blasty wind comes first and stiffens us)
will you step in front of it by some
sleepwalking whim?

Nature's anti-depressants:
some trees, blue blue blue
a three-legged dog
running as if on four,
a pet pigeon on the windowsill,
feet planted on the tired old clay of its own shit,
or a lone goat, tethered to a field it eats tidy,

skies and delicious rain
there on brain's doorstep.
Wordsworth climbed Mt Snowdon,
setting off at couching-time to meet
the climbing sun
'forehead bent Earthward, as if in opposition set
against an enemy'.

Stepping up,
grimly, grimily out of primordial self,
bearing what can't be left,
skull's cargo, hellbent thoughts.
What does he want?
To survive, a wandering human,
by some 'fit converse with the spiritual world'.

Nature his accomplice.
To climb a mountain is to climb himself.
His childhood is a looming rock,
silently glided towards
by the man remembering,
the child approaching,
then one or the other or both

oaring away in terror.
He cannot know who stole the boat.
'There was a boy',
he mutters to himself.
Nothing much happens.
The naked moon
pleases with a tricky light, the mist

rears up and writhes
its 'ocean' about his shoes.
His mind, greedy,
opens its trap.
Magician, he breathes free
the soul he keeps chained
like an animal inside him.

Spring

When gazing upon seas rich in dolphins, make a white
shirt pop with statement bangles. Alone
and sad? Miu Miu's silk loungewear makes the perfect holiday
companion. Be wild with Gucci's rock-
abilly frock, or tease in Vuitton's sky-blue hotpants,
but harken to the mutton-meter.
When wearing the new cocoon skirts do not let your knees
hatch their ageing butterflies. Hike up
nude tights over tucked-in sweaters and let them peek out
from above low-riding skirts. Soften
the severity of a nuclear winter with instantly
lifting playground brights. Oh where is last
year's snow? If your days of azure have forgotten you,
look out for bejewelled styles, or heighten
after-hours looks with gunmetal glitter. Navy blue
suggests intelligence, debate or
challenge. You'll love these star and dove-shaped balloons, made from
biodegradable plastic. Lip-
stick red, French blue, sunflower yellow, psycho florals, stripes,
polka dots: these all have springtime joy.

The Weatherboard at Menzies Creek

The painted partrich lyes in every field,
And, for thy messe, is willing to be kill'd. Jonson, 'To Penshurst'

You, Peter, showing me how to build
a bonfire expertly,
miraculous as a Monet haystack,
the rubbish ordered (loved) into form:
the ten-year-old holiday farm lad
near Salisbury in Wiltshire

sixty years ago, learning in a single day
to make a rick. Apprentice at dawn,
master at noon, knowing exactly
the pitch and catch, you shrank
time into workshape, small mastery of matter
loosening the spirit:

the flame rapidly, thinly
teething up through an igloo
of ash, and smoke steadily
shuffling outwards, not sideways to neighbours
but out across the valley to the clear
space your stark cypresses guard.

The local animals aren't suiciding
into your hands. But, fluent in the semiotics
of the French butcher's window's
'beef anthology', you could use
'every part, except the hair in the ear',
almost justifying the kill.

If sick or self-engulfed when I come here,
my devils are deflected
by a stronger joy:
yours and Nóirín's, who, closing seventy,
left Cardiff to marry you here. Beloved
as a woman out of Hardy,

she matches you in gusto and attack;
keeps viable this humble living.
The morning bread
swells in the truck-red aga,
your making hands
smoulder through arthritis.

Trampolining

for Chris

The fattest eternity is childhood,
minutes stuffed with waiting
and the just-there world
deferred to an afterlife of joy
where magically we outgrow
what could tell us what to do:

we sat cross-legged on the floor, quiet
as the glad-wrapped biscuits on the supper-table,
a summer school-night boiling over
with nightmare prayers
in somebody's Adelaide livingroom,
fed air by a cooler on rollers,

our pastor bellowing at the helm,
hell's ore in his flame-cheeks.
Gorby, Reagan and Thatcher went
chasing round his head with bombs:
explode the world and bring
the roaring-back of God-the-parent!

The grown-ups stamped their thonged
and sandalled feet on the carpet:
the mortgages and what they worked for,
the chip pan bubbling every night at six,
the hand-me-downs all forced to fit:
oh take it Satan, it's all yours . . .

Any day we'd be whooshed up to heaven;
and the kids at school, their parents,
cousins, dogs,
sucked up and funnelled
into hell's gated suburb, far out
where no public transport would travel.

But my brother and I were saving up
for a trampoline: its coming required
every cent of our faith
that we might be allowed to remain
in the human world a bit longer,
to have it and jump on it: to believe

in the leaden feet sunk in the cool summer grass,
the springy canopy shooting us up
above the apple trees, all day and well into dusk,
touching heaven with our hair,
our tongues, our fingertips, then sommersaulting,
shrieking and tumbling

back down into the miracle, or whatever
it was: the thing not yet taken, the present-tense,
cast off by the adults for the kids to play with.

The Poem

One doesn't want to end up
like one's mother.
(One says 'end up'
as if that would be the end.)
Mother never wanted
to be like her mother,
nor did her mother nor hers . . .
You shall inherit,
the mother-mother spirit says.

Whether or not
one becomes a mother
(in the end),
mothers
exist for daughters as surely as the hills,
being both hill and hill-shadow
there with the sun,
cosying up with the night.

They will come with helpful tea,
digestive scones,
years of advice,
anxiety that unravels like intestines
to cover 60 tennis courts,
splendid as a family fleece
inscribed with gems for every worry,
every joy, every how-to-muster-love.

And no mother is wholly mother.
That is the splinter: the still-there self
longing to be other, to be whatever
new thing a child is meant to be.
I dreamt I looked after
my child-mother in the park,
marvellous little likeness
with the family violet eyes:
how foolishly she trusted me,

not knowing how I'd change her,
not seeing how my fingerprint glowed
already on her forehead.

Not being a mother,
I wonder where my spirit will go.
Perhaps into that aged blue that sometimes
is the sky.
The instant my grandmother died,
in another city,
I fell into bed with a god-splitting headache.
Later learning of her death, I went outside
teeming with her secrets,
wrestling with the little mad gene-parcelled demons
that light up the brain and
harrow-vanquish the soul.

The Poet at Ten

The flamingoes at the zoo were kin to her:
their long absurd pink legs . . .
She would stand before the mirror and swivel
her pigeon-toed feet a hundred-
and-eighty degrees inwards.
The knees kinked, each splayed limb
perpetually trying to walk towards the other.
She was 'pretty' but loved to be ugly.

Through the alien schoolyard she ran,
not tripping on her large feet.
Lunchtime was a wavepool of noises:
she'd strain to decipher
what sound burned in the centre of that roar.
The rule-bound games of other children
made no sense to her.
Often she roamed at large,
scowling in her platinum mop,
telling the story of herself to herself.
She was an orphan,
a brave child in wartime England, raising
her ickly baby sister in a barn.

The bullies huddled by the portable:
those she feared and didn't fear, who feared her.
She walked slowly past them,
and they rose as if hypnotised, unable to resist
aping her, wrenching their own feet
painfully inwards.

That year the surgery: the twisted femurs
were broken and straightened.

For seven weeks, on a plywood platform
tied to the wheelchair, the plastered legs
stuck out in front,
she was an island.

She loved her stigmatising pain,
four-inch hooks
neatly seamed among her bones, as if in a diagram.

On dry Autumn school-days,
at home, she wheeled herself around the garden,
a nineteenth-century invalid
coaxing the small fox terrier
to pull her chair like a team of greyhounds,
or Sit! while she read him
I Can Jump Puddles.

Motionless in bed,
under thirty hand-made cards
from children scarcely missed,
she tried to feel the bones 'knitting'.

After three months,
two operations,
she would learn to walk again,

legs transfigured,
corrected for the world.
Brown and spindly at first,
skin peeling and mottled, yellow and blue,
she would step like a baby bird.

Her near future perfect self,
a blonde Californian teenage goddess
with an effortless mastery of slang,
loped and pranced along a beach in Adelaide.

Frames

The bright rosy faces of those people –
inhabiting their place, the moment
without fear,
as if they lived in hives
of love continuous
as gas hot water, and flowed

through seamless days and had
no reason to suspect themselves.
Solid worlds,
where solid things are good.
The faces sheet,
the eyes look past.

How to keep hold of a self
so frangible, so often breaking up
and coming back together,
a living mosaic,
a small piece of wood,
a hide-house of hair.

~

Flying over the old leather surface of the sea:
changing and not-changing,
a slow holding-together
of desolate parts, thoughts rapid
as geckoes flicking
in and out of the mind's story.

Density of clouds,
boiling crystal,
something rumbling
and beginning
in the one silence, the human engine
in the plane's roar.

The unmatched spines of hills
spread like cattle.
You unpick the bones
of a stream, then a river,
widely, bluely
opening into larger blues, layered in
an immensity of air.

~

A heart-unfurling peace:
the loudness
and largeness of the waves,
and the eye-breaking brightness –
all that there is!

In order to stem the slow internal bleeding
of grief, or illness,
the thing
that thieves away silence –
fall down here like a shipwreck,

you ungraspable soul:
for you truth changes
like sand underfoot,
this moment a coffin,
the next a hope that sails.

A lizard squeezes
through the long grasses;
briefly its head,
golden, fat, pulsating
in gentle riveted joy.

All the world rivets the mind:
do not wrest yourself
from this, the day,
intent as a story to be learned,
while there is time.

Notes for the time being

How many sonnets must we write
before the great gong sounds in Heaven? Peter Porter

Relieved like a criminal
at last apprehended
and tricked out of daylight.
Will I be you again?

Too much freedom
is not enough.
How large or small the world
where time fits.

Terrible thing a head
from which no thought escapes.
As the world said
good-bye to you

it grew small and glazy,
a thing seen beneath tears
as when a child says good-bye
to a too-much-trouble pet.

~

Soul frees itself
(from something),
or tries to imagine
it gone, the heavy –

still carrying
what's precious
– the gold, the old –
and the fuse hope.

Thrown into light, thrown into dark,
etc. Where does illness live,
what does it want?
And sits before the Sybil,

begging for speech.
Describe your fear.
How do you feel out of 10?
Out of 9?

~

Soul is confused, sad for no reason,
can't remember;
sits in her chair and stares
like someone much older
who'll never again remember.

Weeps, as if out of the corner
of humanity's loose mouth;
her tears are lost coins, spilling down
the loud spiral of that machine,
somewhere in eternity, that codes them:

Grief 1, Grief 2, and
how unusual: Griefs 11 and 19.
And sometimes, of course, there is joy,
also for no reason – here you ask
what has reason got to do with it? –

To William Drummond at Hawthornden

O sacred solitude, divine retreat,
Choice of the prudent, envy of the great!
By the pure stream, or in the waving shade
I court fair Wisdom, that celestial maid.

There from the ways of man, laid safe ashore
I smile to hear the distant tempest roar.
There, happy, and with business unperplexed,
This life I relish and secure the next.

Edward Young: plaque at Hawthornden Castle

1.

The house its own silence: walls of deep thick stone,
jammed once with books of every language,
and outside, more stone, then lyric forest,
cliffs, mossed paths, a semi-moat of Esk,
conspiring a glutful solitude.

2.

I half expect the short-plod
nineteen-stone steps of Ben Jonson,
'dessembler of ill parts which raigne in him',
in the second shoes that carried him from London.
'He said to me that I was too good and simple,

3.

and that oft a mans modestie made a fool
of his wit.' You wrote down all he said
(little that you said), braggings, gossip,
words that flew into the hermit's house,
caught and dried like strips of herring.

4.

You lacked athletic stuff for all-night talk,
and snuffed the garrulous guest
with a bedtime taper that he ferried, still speaking,
into the swallowing dark, leaving you alone
to inspect your stranger-altered state.

5.

Poems: Amorous, Funerall, Divine,
requiting privity with every-kind verse:
public tears for the public prince, then
for your private love, the terribly young
sweet woman dead before the wedding:

6.

going indoors to fathom out the aspects
of a loss-devoured soul, 'laid safe ashore'
from all the world that strains to godspeed joy.
All night I hear the barn owls calling
each other, or their own insistent phantoms.

7.

They are not calling me, but I am tensed,
listening to their stern goodnights,
long as sleep that Macbeth murdered
when he claimed his own gigantic solitude,
leaping onto that chunk of immortality

8.

he was not allowed and could not endure.
I dream too often of some familiar corpse
that once long ago I must have killed, covered
and leapt from, into the largest life,
too filled with gifts I have not strength to use.

9.

Through the window the sloping slate roof
tinges with green slime, ancient and luminous
in rain almost continuous, a conversation
we come into the midst of, as if
time does not pass but waits,

10.

always out of reach and always near, overleaping
itself in the mind. My attic here like
that room of dream-recur, some sleep-discovered
nook we never knew existed, that opens
and greets us like the life I don't dare.

Alpacas

The cria had been born early, the owner not yet
aware, not there to supervise, inspect,
to be farmer or man. The cria was there,

new, staggering, abrupt;
its comprehension already filled-up with a universe,
this fleece-producing field bordered by a driveway,

where elders were standing around, teaching it stillness:
mother blood and awe, the others half-looking
over their shoulders, seeming nonchalantly private.

Visit

i.m. B.L., SJ

Visiting your brother, the priest, in hospital,
he may be dying, coughing blood, they
don't know why. His legs leak, he has lost jolly fat.
Alone, half-naked in the public ward,
he greets us: one dainty leg drawn over the other,
face luminous, eyes lively;
not saying 'why this suffering',
just present, like a character in a fresco,
man with blood bucket. Humanly
getting-on-with-it, he hacks into the stainless
steel and shows us 'rather red as you can see'.

A Baby

'Poor neurons!', your mother cries,
cradling your barely-yet brain that grabs
being from all she says and is.

Months back, learning of your female sex,
she wept for fear that all she feared
within herself would then be yours.

Now fearlessly born you pull at a breast
as big as your head, filling yourself with all that there is,
making your mother almost another.

Beauty

I stepped into Beauty, this was it: islands,
mountains, water, clouds and sky.
Not the street in blossom

or autumn leaf, or the dog in winter leaping
at the window, but Beauty raging
because we knew it to be.

Then I slipped back to the usual, the time-too-fast,
the life I crave to love more truly
than any mountain could surmise.

The Couple who Own the Lebanese Café

Each morning except Tuesday for twenty years he rises
at four to go to the market.
Each day they are there in their shop,
she, impossibly sexy in loud tight dresses,
casually turning the skewers,
he outside, soberly drinking
with the regulars.

Behind the counter they dance around each other,
as if they are building and re-building up love
that washes away each night
as love must, falling under the tide, dissolving
in the heart of the farthest star, to be reborn
entirely through human effort,
the smallest gestures, the brighest capsicums.

Debtor's Prison

Do not look for the future, it is gone,
tossed away clean as a wish-bone
over the shining shoulder of a dragon
with oh! the silver clogs we now repent,
those credit cards we spent to space like rockets:
the past-tense will heavy our shallow pockets.

Same old same old. And the snark present-tense
cares for itself and will not cleanse
out our wounds like a loving fellow cat.
Use what strength you can to sorry-smile
at tomorrow's better woman, who all the while
flexes her teeth and can't help but regret you.

Holiday

Behold, I shew you a mystery; We shall not all sleep, but we shall all be changed . . . I Corinthians 15:51

for Kate

We stride into the white waves like kings.
We who demand perfection
of ourselves and the world, we proclaim
the height of the spray to be flawless,
this sky immortal.

We surge on the breast of life as it should be,
no rocks or seaweed or monsters,
our glad heads thrown about,
luminous and singing. Later we talk
of what must be repaired: the severed self,

its open wires of longing,
its childish hand grasping for care.

The Beautiful Lines

How wrongly I tried to describe the lines
my friend saw under her eyes, on her twenty-ninth birthday –
'But they are barely there – like birds
that haven't landed yet!' A sinister image, capturing nothing.

But she only wanted them gone, talked of eye-cream
that calls itself 'age-defying'.
These mortal marks of mortality:
is it morbid to love them?

The Gone

We turn them to stone when they go.
(It is always them and us
with the dead.)
They have mostly been dead
too long still to be mourned.
The tilting graves are exhibitions
built up inside: here are parents,
children and grandchildren,
flat-packed into the present *here lie*
and the single past tense of the headstone.
They have slipped beyond family
and twinkle anonymously
in the magical DNA that lies
about like powder at the edge of things.
But our own dead are everywhere.
Closing our eyes at night,
we imagine ourselves like them,
perhaps in a zone where forever
we might freeze, or a sea
or river we swim for all durations.
They tour that multiplex
of wherever-we-think-them-to-be:
shadowing us to work, leaping onto the bus,
standing by the filing cabinet, chatting.
Something about existence
insists on presence.

The dead, surely they just want life again,
and it is there:
haunting them up to their eaves,
clinging to their hands like ropes of ghost-cloth,
vexing their spoon drawers,
blitzing their screens with images.

Description of a Ritual

Freeling Cemetery, SA – i.m. Valda Ince, 1935–2008

Life a mere flash, or flesh –
coins-as-headlights winking in the daylight,
and we are all in Charon's dinghy.
Our creeping vehicles fog up
with family gossip: then our car-sized groups
dissolve into a clan, semi-strangers with like faces,
attending the secular comforts of religion.
Nobody is damned or redeemed.

We're flowers that open and shut, we endure
shiftily in memory. And the dead
have afterlife in local habitation and a name.
This place she chose for herself, the burial
modelled on her friend's, last Winter – the cemetery
fringed with cypresses and a caravan park,
its modest frontier of headstones
facing out miles of unborn suburbs.

Her graveside is formal as a picnic, a row of chairs
along the edge for those who will most
weep, her grandmother-daughters,
seeding her down with tears
a water-holding grave can hold. They are bowed
by afterlove that the dead, leaving the world's cold,
drape around the living like a coat,
but the sons and grandsons, flanked behind them,

bearded and pony-tailed,
are inscrutable as the Pictish ancestors
we may or may not share. Green slithering hoists
unravelling to its fathom, its *this-far-no-further,*
the coffin goes one finite down,
and a pungent, non-descript hell
remains above, digesting *love-never-enough*,
embryo losses hatching in the open air.

Adopted to child a marriage, she
knitted herself into new blood,
then seven came by birth.
She was their principal Sister from the elsewhere
of First, keeper of all goodness and terror.
Her toddler brothers shadowed her to school,
she smuggled them in and fed them
what she knew of the world.

And in death she is adopted again, the first
(as an adult) to die. Her ageing brothers and sisters
carry and bury her, their own in words of stone,
and scattered in anecdotes.
How glad she would be to zip away,
gripping the wheel with hungry speed
as my father does, for once at peace with GPS,
the slightly-rights and worldly lefts.

Portobello

Edinburgh

The stupid calm surprise of it, there
at the end of a long bus ride through cliffs
of tenements, not all charming or sandstone,
two old ladies chatting quietly behind me,
'so many cars for sale along one street: why?'
This strand, the plaque says, had its hey-day:
once was sunlight, Punch and Judy shows,
sand-clad children and bathing-boxed mothers –

the seriousness of outings! All swept up and gone
where childhood goes.
The people here now are pieces of the sea.
Unordered by any god, they sift through their element
as if they have no days to count,
the way we do at the end of the world.

Blue Above the Chimneys

Christine Marion Fraser's
autobiography, I found
in a second-hand bookshop
in Kelvinbridge, Glasgow.
Christine's father, as my aunt
recently discovered,
was my great-grandfather,
who had had a second family
in his sixties: none of our
business, perhaps.
I grew up knowing nothing
much about his son, my dead
grandfather, Alexander. They say he was tall,
and liked to draw and write stories,
was a bully and a drinker
who often fell apart.
He left Glasgow in his youth,
settled in Adelaide, never
returned to visit, and in 1960 died young
of a heart-attack, in Melbourne,
leaving seven children and a wife.
Around the same time,
his father, John Fraser, at sixty or so,
a widower, married a widow:
they had five children,
Christine the eldest, and they lived
in near poverty, in a stark grey tenement.
He worked in a Glasgow shipyard,

drank, and could be violent,
gruff, steely, also tender.
Christine describes him
as bird: 'his iron-grey head
sticking out from our kitchen
window one flight up, his eagle eyes
raking through the tumbling throng
in a search for his brood of four'.
His hands were 'horny' and 'hard'.
His wife, Evelyn, died at fifty-two
of 'weariness', and he shortly after,
at eighty-one, of grief for her.

In Glasgow, my eagle eyes
raked through the streets
(nothing 'tumbling', no throng –
quiet, slow-curving crescents).
In so many Scottish faces and voices,
a toughness, a cheerful grimness,
as with my relatives or me.
But there was no-one in this city
that I knew, and I was happy not to know
who I was related to.
There must be a point when family,
foreign as ancestors,
is not family: all the threads
of distance and doubleness let go
into a human larger narrative.

Christine's world overlaps
mine and my Aunt's, mainly for the early story
of how my grandfather may have been,
if he was anything like his father.

Imagination

The air was always cramped with miracles.
The church, or 'assembly', would gather
in a grand old theatre: the pastors
emerging one by one from deep red curtains
to take their seven seats onstage,
a chorus line of suited legs.
My family were new recruits (I was seven)
snapped from a life of sin to cancel beer
and swim in the crowd of converts
who called each other 'Brother'
and 'Sister', 'Aunty' and 'Uncle'
– the lie kept me spellbound.

There were tales of cancer
diminished to a pea by prayer,
addicts dropping their needles and singing.
Proof of God was always needed
by believers. Miracles
made life worth having, each subject
struck by God as by lightning.
Heaven delayed, we roamed together
for sundry salvagable souls
in the wrecked world's wreck.
My ten-year-old friend Sarah
got a cancer that was stronger

than faith: her leg with its large knot
was amputated. The night before that
the whole assembly shouted
and prayed for the cancer to die,
her leg to be saved. Oblivious
to a thousand prayers preying on her leg,
pre-operative, she was deep in a scarcely
imaginable childhood bravery, imagining
how she'd learn to walk again,
her artificial leg thrown sideways and forth
with each dancing step, a survivor,
a jaunty jagged figure in brazen health.

The Orchardist

Renmark, South Australia (Riverland)

In the bitten dusk, his lemons
gleamed their own light, too much, too rich for harvest.
He was blacklisted, we later learned, for cheating workers,
the wretched flesh, unpredictable as weather,
he hated to need. Two kids aged 9 and 10 had spidered
words in Romanian on the bedroom wall
in the derelict fruitpickers' house.

At night we walked the river, following its curves
that wound us out to where a redgum
stood marooned at water's edge, fossilised in thirst;
a sliver of silver still flashing
in the cavernous bed, eluding, for now,
the underground stealthwork of pipes tugging the river
out of itself, into the ticking sprinklers.

At dawn we were into the fragrant avenues of citrus,
dreamily caught in the strangeness of labour.
Throwing our ladders on the mass of a laden tree,
lunging blind into the leaves, we learned
by hand instead of heart; our finger-muscles
rippling up, reaching and grabbing, tearing the fruit
from its branch as if from a painting.

All day the farmer circled on his tractor, mad as a bull-rider,
lurching on thick dry mud-tracks braided yesterday
and yesterday, shouting *Truck coming tomorrow!*
as if to say, *The end of the world!* On our last day
his neighbours mushroomed in the avenues
to help; sauntering past us, he glinted in defiance: *I hire*
a million dollars and grow this up from nothing!

Public Service

Our lost skulls orbit one another
in their fleshfolds, in the office's
daylight-eating light. We are here
to be here, reliable as mustard.
Work smoulders
a not quite urgent urgency
– human voices quench it,
my colleagues, my brothers!

Our voices grind the air, our tales
are the tales of the world, boyfriends
shovelling backyards for love,
self-jeers of too-skinny, too-fat.
We know our place
in the hierarchy of weight.
'The meaning of work?'
It makes us a mask, a shell,
builds a house, it is ours.

My job is this: I research the ways
for a government to intervene
and adjust human trajectories.
For hours I've read how our brains
in infancy are worlded:
forests of voices, the moving light
touching and tickling us,
the love that sets us,
never to change, forever.
We are made by what loves us,
our thought-paths grooved by the terrible
thumbs of those who try their best.

Adults, barely changeable,
we long for change, that quick
suddenness in the brain.
Here we think ourselves wasted,
stepping each day off the elevator
into a desert, a day-world, farcing
a whole-world, we'd retrieve right now
if we could change our job:
in our heads at night, that story
in our veins, its reality
strong as the branch that scrapes
the guttering when we sleep.

24TH FLOOR

The desk is pushed up facing the window.
Sleepless lights, dry voices, partitions shielding none.
Then silence after 5,

an absurd desire to seize the day, too late.
Invisible the turtley Dandenongs,
ninety-three minutes of cruel traffic hence,

never not there, never closer:
the desk like a plane that doesn't land,
the day only pretending to end.

I hear, still, a colleague's bitter curses, tirelessly
at the system's recurring red letters saying 'Error'
– human passion authentic as phlegm,

clinging to the air's contagions and my own
festering cold, a migrant
from that desk over there, proof of connection.

The cheap building rattles with winter
storming the glassy streets below,
all wind and little rain, and more than weather:

something else, some dampness of the mind
that spreads and seals a comforting alienation.
The unfelt rain a fury of scratches on silver.

Second Ode

Wordsworth is far from the grave
of his daughter. Surprised by joy –
not of his being: a transport;
something carries him.

From A to B, just fleetingly,
out of grief's bog,
he doubles, triples, whirls on the spot:
joy, sorrow at joy that can't be shared,

guilt at joy's split-second song.
Oh heart, that some
vicissitude has found:
we have climbed this far, and where next?

New Year's Eve

Our picnic on the beach pinned down by food.
A wind-dark sea
is all but people-swept, just an incandescent white-
sailed boat stealthing outwards: out to where, to where?
Where weather comes from, always 'out there'.
The boat is gliding swiftly out, its sails a steeple,
it means to change, to come back new,
its people cheer-filling its sails.
At the tear in the year,
the storm getting closer, the hungry new year
furrowing in, the boat forging out, it happens:
the dark needling rain comes sideways,
we see the sailboat steadfastly sailless in the gale
sailing back to our shared shore.

Notes

Ode to Coleridge: Quotations are from Wordsworth's *The Prelude.*

Spring: This poem has some phrases from British *Vogue* and *Harpers Bazaar.*

To William Drummond at Hawthornden: Quotations in the poem are from Drummond's *Conversations*, which recorded Ben Jonson's visit in the winter of 1618-19.

Alpacas: A cria is a baby alpaca.

Blue Above the Chimneys: This is the title of an autobiography by Christine Marion Fraser, published by Hutchinson in 1980.

Poetry in print from John Leonard Press

2006	
A bud	*Claire Gaskin*
Cube Root of Book	*Paul Magee*
Ocean Island	*Julian Croft*
The Passion Paintings: Poems 1983-2006	*Aileen Kelly*
2007	
Vertigo | a cantata |	*Jordie Albiston*
The Incoming Tide	*Petra White*
Letters to the Tremulous Hand	*Elizabeth Campbell*
Man Wolf Man	*L K Holt*
2008	
Poems 1980-2008	*Jan Owen*
White Knight with Bee Box: New and Selected Poems	*Peter Steele*
Growing Up with Mr Menzies	*John Jenkins*
Therapy Like Fish: New and Selected Poems	*Marcella Polain*
2009	
Collected Poems	*Vincent Buckley* ed. *Chris Wallace-Crabbe*
The sonnet according to 'm'	*Jordie Albiston*
White camel	*Morgan Yasbincek*
Pilbara	*Mark O'Connor*
Marriage for Beginners	*Catherine Bateson*
2010	
The Simplified World	*Petra White*
Patience, Mutiny	*L K Holt*
Phantom Limb	*David Musgrave*

JOHN LEONARD PRESS